Sinner Man

PAUL McCULLEY

To Joe

Blessings your friend

Paul

What Others are Saying

"This book demonstrates how, with the right influences, a kid in trouble can become a positive role model for others."
— Mike De Wine, U. S. Senator

"**Sinnerman** is a tale of one person's journey – a journey of courage with valuable lessons for all of us."
— Rob Portman, U. S. Congressman

"I started reading **Sinnerman** and couldn't put it down."
— Sam Bateman
Ohio State Representative

"A heart wrenching account of how transformation takes place in a person's life."
— Rev. Damon Lynch Jr.
President, Baptist Ministers Conference of Cincinnati

"**Sinnerman** should be required reading for everyone – especially teenagers!"
— Hope Taft, Director
Ohio Parents for Drug Free Youth

DEDICATION

This book is dedicated to the
grace of God, my children
Paula, Kevin, and Lauri,
and my wife, Retta.

Timeline

Ages 13 -25   30 Arrests

7 Workhouse Sentences

3 Imprisonments in Army Stockade

Age 13   First Arrest, Assault

& Battery, Truancy

Age 15   Three Court Martials, U.S. Army

Age 20   Six Months in Alcoholic Ward

Age 29   MINISTER

After Accepting Christ

— Age 29 minister

— 27 years pastor

— 3 years evangelist

— Trustee National Drug Task Force

— Founder, Starting Point, motivational seminars for at risk youth – low income – incarcerated

— Clermont Co. Corrections Board, Ohio

— Clermont Co. Family & Children First Cabinet, Ohio

Story broadcast all over the world
in 39 languages through the radio
program *Unshackled!*

CHAPTER 1

COWARD AND THE COCKROACH

CHAPTER 1

COWARD AND THE COCKROACH

In most ways, it was just the morning after another drunken spree—another arrest by city cops and another wake-up in solitary confinement. But this one was to be different.

I was on a concrete slab, just big enough to lie on. As I raised up on one side I saw it—a giant cockroach. They grow 'em big in a Cincinnati jail, what with jailhouse food and coffee and all. This was at least two inches long and was crawling up toward me from a crack.

It seemed like I might have been having a nightmare. But a man has to sink pretty low to be scared of a cockroach. I was terrified. Fear completely possessed me as I realized I had no place to run. I jumped up. A second later I was pounding on the cell door and screaming, "Let me out of here!" If it hadn't been near court time they wouldn't have paid any attention to me. But the turnkey was just on his way to get me. He unlocked the cell, and I moved out in a hurry.

The ugliness of that cockroach and the way I panicked when he started up out of the crack was frozen on my mind. Even worse was the cowardliness of my fright. My mind was tormented as the realization of my despicable condition came over me.

"Paul McCulley, is this the way you are going to spend the rest of your life? In and out of jail? From one drunk to the next? Always on the run?" It was almost as if I was preaching to myself.

From the bullpen I joined the parade through the courtroom. The judges handed me 10 days this time. The paddy wagon was full of men, packed too tight to move more than an inch or two.

When we reached the workhouse, I was sick of the whole mess. Sick of jail, sick and tired of being a bum; just fed up. Conditions were poor in the workhouse, very poor. They averaged about 500 prisoners a day, mostly for public drunkenness.

I couldn't remember anything from the night before. It was later, after my release, that one of my drinking buddies filled in the missing pieces. Bill said we had been soaking it up for weeks; months really. We went from one bottle of wine to the next. Thunderbird on The Rocks, they called it.

I spent my days bumming in the streets and my nights sleeping like a few other of my friends; in junk autos, laundromats, viaducts, hallways, and just about anywhere a bum could hide from the cops.

One of the guys had an apartment and sometimes we could get a meal there. Sometimes we would go to my sister's place. But food didn't really matter. It was wine we wanted and needed. Only the bottle could dissolve our problems.

Bill was about my age. I was 25. He might have been a year older. We kept pretty clean by using the showers in the community pools. We would take a shower with our clothes on, wash them, hang around until our garments dried, and then went back to the streets to burn a few more coins.

Between September 1958 and September 1963, I had been in the workhouse seven times. The cops had picked me up a few times between 1953 and 1963 for assault and battery along with the public drunkenness charges. I had paid about 25 fines during that period for charges ranging from being drunk to assault. There were a lot of other crimes, robbery and the like, which the cops didn't know about.

The night before my last arrest we went to a restaurant to eat. I was so drunk and all full of "bennies" I was falling over myself. I tried to make out with two girls sitting by themselves, but they paid no attention. I cussed them out—called them every name in the book—I remembered that part later. The rest only Bill and the cops knew.

I walked out and sat on a step until I fell over and rolled into the gutter. I was half in the gutter, half on the sidewalk when the police came by. Next thing I knew I woke up in the hole. That's when that cockroach crawled toward me.

Many times before, I had closed my eyes and seen snakes, skeletons, and weird faces. This is a common experience for drunks the morning
after. But this time I knew fear as I had never experienced it before.

Paul McCulley had reached the end of the line. This was the end. One way or another, it had to end. But where had it all begun? How did I ever hit bottom? My mind reached back to the neighborhood, the old gang, and that time I first went wrong.

CHAPTER 2

STARTED BY "PLAYING HOOKY"

CHAPTER 2

STARTED BY "PLAYING HOOKY"

Every person faces at one time or another a choice of roads. Mine came when I was in the 5th grade. I was a good student with a record of "A's" and "S's."

My older brother, who was about 13, was playing hooky and tried to persuade me to go with him as we walked toward school. I left him in a little delicatessen after telling him to wait. I really had no intention of going back to meet him or of skipping classes that day.

My homeroom teacher, a kind lady, had asked me to see her before class. She had some used clothing to give me, and being from an 8th and State family of very poor means, the clothes were appreciated.

But on the way to her room another teacher spotted me and chased me from the building for violating the "no one in the halls before school" rule. She really yelled and laid it on the line. As a result, I walked out of the building, threw up my hands and said "the heck with it."

I went to find my brother. As we walked along, we came to the fork in the road where

I made the turn away from authority and understanding of adult leadership. We took the route leading away from school, and for two solid weeks played hooky. When we were caught and punished, he ran away, was captured, and sent to a home for boys.

We managed well during our "vacation" from school; spending most of the time in my brother's girlfriend's apartment. When the girl and her mother had left for the day I was boosted by my brother's strong arms to the transom. I climbed in where it was no trick to open the door. We lived it up, enjoying free food and a comfortable setup until just before they were due to return. Then, after cleaning up the evidence of our having been there, we locked the door behind us and headed home with the other neighborhood kids as they went home from school.

Between the 5th and 8th grades, I was completely different. It was a struggle to go to school and I continued to play hooky. I could make 90-95 without even trying on my tests, but I just lost all interest. I just went to get away and felt I was running from an unknown "something."

Somehow, I knew I was mean and dirty inside. But I didn't have the slightest idea of what to do about it; I didn't really care. That first day I took the wrong fork in the road, I started a downhill course and before it was over I was bound to hit bottom. One thing might have prevented my life of trouble, but I had forgotten it as soon as it happened.

A fellow who lived next door to us had started an interdenominational church and he took our family to services with him. I had gone to the altar at the age of five after feeling sorry for my sins. I remember I had picked on a little girl about three years old and my meanness weighed on my mind. I felt really good after going to the altar, but the feeling left as I walked out of the church door. A lot was to happen in the almost 20 years before this experience was to be brought to my mind again.

Sin was a way of life around 8th and State. Our neighborhood was made of the ugliness and filthy moral conditions most folks just read about. There wasn't much chance we'd turn out anything but rotten.

I was in the 8th grade when our family moved to Barbourville, Kentucky. The elementary school there was in an old, but sturdy building. I had a very nice teacher, Miss Kathy Wilson. She was a good-looking lady with a warm, outgoing personality. Miss Wilson was nice to everybody, but her kindness to me didn't prevent me from playing hooky on and off.

When she confronted me one day about skipping classes, I told her I had been home sick. She then related that the truant officer had been to my home and she knew I was lying.

Miss Wilson tried to get me out of my seat to paddle me, but I hung on to the seat with both hands. She swung the board, but hit only the desk. I made a dash for the door, but she was quicker, getting there the same time that I did, and grabbed my right arm. As I swung my arm with all its youthful energy, her face hit into the wall. As she fell to the floor with blood running from her mouth, I jumped through an open window.

Later a cop drove by alongside me and two buddies later as we were on our way back from Harlan. When they questioned us, I said my name was Hammick—my mother's maiden name—and they drove off. Things were getting a little too hot and I decided to leave town.

I went to the highway and started hitchhiking. My luck lasted only until the second ride when a cop, on his way to Corbin to telegraph Cincinnati police, picked me up. He didn't have his hat on and this kept me from recognizing him until I was inside the car. His anger inspired the promise, "When I get you back to town, I'll take my belt off and beat the dickens out of you."

Paul McCulley had moved down that road toward the life of a criminal—charged at age 13 with assault and battery.

CHAPTER 3

ASKING FOR TROUBLE

CHAPTER 3

ASKING FOR TROUBLE

The cops locked me in the Knox County jail where I awaited a trial before the juvenile judge on charges of assault and battery. One sure way to make a young criminal worse is to throw him together with older, more experienced hoods. I gained quite an education during my week in that cell.

Twelve men, all waiting for the grand jury, shared that cage. One of the guys was in for rape and headed for a sure rap in the pen. He uttered a lewd remark as the jailer was turning the key behind me.

Only the other prisoners, who still had some scruples left, protected me from the advances of this sex fiend. The experience I gained during that confinement was to prove valuable later on as the years ahead were filled with many encounters with such demented characters.

The judge listened to my record of truancy and smashing Miss Wilson into the wall. He put me on probation for an indefinite period. The next day I stole $5 from my mother's dress pocket and hopped a bus for Cincinnati.

An older sister and her husband took me in. They were swell to me, and with the approval of my folks, accepted my legal guardianship. Their devout Catholic lives and their influence no doubt helped to somewhat counteract the teaching I had received on the street.

About two years later, I went to stay with my parents again, having finished my 8th grade studies. Then, with my older brother's birth certificate in my pocket, I started hitchhiking to Florida with Skeeter, a 19-year-old-friend.

We had reached Knoxville when we were struck with the bright idea of enlisting in the Army. I became a soldier on my 15th birthday, using a birth certificate which stated I was 18.

Skeeter had a little trouble making it. They required a man to weigh 105 pounds and he tipped the scales at 100. A sergeant sent Skeeter out to get fifty cents worth of bananas. After gulping these down, he weighed 104. They then sent for five or six bottles of water. It was a sick-looking Skeeter who made the grade a short time later weighing 105. He went to Fort Gordon for basic and training as an MP.

They held me at Fort Jackson where we had both been processed. During basic training, I was constantly in trouble and the instructors stayed on my back. I made sharpshooter with my rifle and passed basic testing with flying colors. But I was a smart-alek with a knack for upsetting everyone around me.

Tests given by the Army showed me a natural for radio communications school. I spent a month absorbing what they had to offer in this line. If I had been inclined to behave myself and play it straight in the service, things might have worked out. But sin has a way of tightening its grip on a kid so he can't take a decent route.

The first time you get in trouble isn't so bad. But after the next, it's a little harder to change. Pretty soon rebellion and contempt for everything worthwhile seemed a perfectly natural way to live.

I should have been proud of the uniform I wore. In a way, I guess I was, but when I went home on leave after radio school, I met a friend who was AWOL form the Marines. He had done a hitch in reform school with my brother.

I went AWOL, too. While we were hanging around the old neighborhood together we ran into two more guys who were AWOL. I had overstayed my leave by 31 days when

Paul McCulley

the cops discovered us sleeping in an old auto.

The other three admitted they were AWOL when they were questioned at this police station. I told them I had been playing hooky so they arrested me for truancy.

I quickly saw I couldn't get out of it this way. When I confessed I was also AWOL they transferred me to the city jail, then to Fort Thomas, where I was to wait a week for a chartered Greyhound prisoner bus. The bus ran weekly from Columbus, Ohio, with prisoners being held at Fort Hayes. It gathered prisoners at Fort Thomas and delivered its load at Fort Knox.

CHAPTER 4

REBELLION IN THE STOCKADE

CHAPTER 4

REBELLION IN THE STOCKADE

One of the prisoners being held at Fort Thomas for the chartered bus had recently made an escape from Fort Knox and was scheming to try it again. His first escape had been accomplished by hiding himself in a wall locker which had been loaded on a truck bound for the outside.

This guy was built pretty small, but he sure knew his way around. He convinced us anyway and we were ready to follow. He figured we could get out of the Fort Thomas prison area by a dash over the hill at supper time.

A car was used to bring food to us from a restaurant on the outside. As we were going out to get our supper from the car, this guy planned that we would throw the food in the driver's face, run off over the hill, and make a clean getaway. But it looked a little too risky for him when the time drew near and he chickened out, saying he would wait for another opportunity.

His attempt came later after we had been transported to the little bullpen at Fort Knox. As our names were being called to go from a small building to be processed, he hid under the building. He had his escape route picked, but the bus driver and a guard happened to be standing in the way. The escape artist was soon missed, caught, and consigned to the hole.

We were sent to reassignment barracks and placed on permanent KP. But the large number of prisoners on hand caused some unexpected complications.

Then came one of the dirtiest deals we saw in service. The court martials were a swift process. After two days under guard, I got a snappy sentence "$50 fine and 30 days suspended."

There were two stockades at Fort Knox, the newest being a modern installation similar to a federal pen. But due to the excess number of prisoners, officials wanted to open the old stockade. We who were on suspended sentences were chosen to help fill it. Armed guards entered our barracks and commanded, "Get your stuff together." Our suspended sentences were no longer suspended.

Crude conditions existed inside the old stockade. They placed us on half rations and we were constantly harassed. Prisoners can stand just so much, and when we reached our limits, we naturally revolted—refusing to do certain things.

Two soldiers went from barrack to barrack with a plot to refuse to fall out for head count after the evening meal. According to plan, everyone stayed in his quarters when the whistle was blown. A few inmates in one barrack were visited by a lieutenant and persuaded to fall out.

When the remaining prisoners saw them on the company street everybody started falling out. I was the last in my barracks to make the move. As I moved toward the door a sergeant urged me to move faster. I tossed my coat aside and told him, "You're stupid" and went back and laid on my bunk.

Next thing I knew the entire company was assembled on the field with me standing far off and faced away. The lieutenant told them I was going to be an example of what happens to fellows when they fail to obey orders.

From there I was taken to the Major's office. He had me placed in solitary confinement where I began waiting for general court martial.

Conditions were very bad. Breakfast consisted of dry cereal; no milk or sugar. "C" ration crackers and lettuce made up the balance of my diet. During the first two days,

I managed to save the crackers from about four meals, looking ahead to when things might get even worse. A guard saw them and flushed them down the toilet.

CHAPTER 5

MILITARY TROUBLEMAKER

CHAPTER 5

MILITARY TROUBLEMAKER

Fourteen days in the hole at Fort Knox was a pretty stiff assignment for a 15-year old, even with an 8th & State background. Sometime about the 9th day I sent for a chaplain and confessed my age to him. The Major then transferred me to a cell containing about 20 other prisoners.

The modern federal-type pen was a big step up over the solitary confinement hole. Meaningless hours passed a bit quicker due to the conversation with other prisoners.

Where there was no trouble, I felt obligated somehow to start it. The other prisoners were out working when a sergeant came by my bunk and ordered me to start polishing my shoes. When he returned a short time later I informed him, "I'm not shining my shoes."

"You're that punk that just got out of solitary, aren't you? Well, I'm going to see the Major and try and get you back in the hole." He kept his word and worked pretty hard on the officer to get me out of circulation again. But the Major, because of my age, refused to send me back to the hole. This further aggravated the sergeant who was very rough on me at every opportunity after that.

When I was assigned to a company for advanced infantry training, I took advantage of the situation and went AWOL again. Military Police officers captured me in Cincinnati and I netted 30 more days in the stockade. After my release, I went AWOL again.

Like a rat seeking his familiar old hole, I headed back to 8th and State and enjoyed a brief time of freedom before I was arrested again. This time I bumped into an MP as he was starting out of our back door and I was just going in.

They handed me another 30 days in Fort Knox stockade at my third court martial and began processing me for a general discharge on honorable conditions. I got off light because I was a minor.

My Army record painted an accurate picture of what I really was on the inside. Out of the 13 months in uniform, I had chalked up 191 bad days.

Some people claim the Army can ruin a man. I don't believe this. Military life only tends to drive a person a little quicker in the direction he's headed. In my case it was downhill all the way. I had picked up a few new tricks in the service, gotten a little meaner, and intensified my compulsion to sin. But it was the same old Paul McCulley who took off an Army uniform and returned to the sin-filled hangouts around 8th and State.

I got all drunked-up one night and was tapping a finger ring on the glass front of a jukebox when a waitress complained. I just stood there and smashed out every glass in the unit.

Three cops responded to the call. As they came toward me, one, in a showoff gesture, threw away his club and reached for me. I let him have a hard punch and the other officers grabbed me. They held me until the first cop hit me—hard enough to knock me through an open doorway. Next thing I knew there were seven of them around me on the street.

"Alright, I'll go," I yelled as I got up and rushed for one of them. My fists were working on him when a billy club came down on my head. When I woke up about two minutes later, I was handcuffed hands behind my back to a parking meter.

In the back of the police car, I cursed the officers and refused to answer questions as we sped toward the jail. When Irish Joe, the turnkey, asked me how old I was I replied

"You're a Dick Tracy, find out for yourself."
He worked me over good and I woke up
feeling I had two heads. Every part of my
body was sore. The judge let me off with
unofficial probation for six months when my
dad appeared in the courtroom.

There wasn't anything I wasn't ready to
do. Dope had a solid grip on the 8th and
State crowd. We started out taking Valo
inhalers and squeezing their contents into
coffee. Bennies were common and this led to
deeper trouble for some of the guys.

Mike, a fine-looking fellow with whom I
had attended Oyler Elementary, was boiling
out paregoric. One night he smashed his
girlfriend's face and broke her nose. While
she was in the emergency room, Mike stole a
needle. He had to steal a lot of other things
to pay for the habit. A conviction of armed
robbery later sent him to Sing Sing.

From October to July 1, I lived the life of
a bum, in one scrape after the other, but
somehow lucky enough to avoid being
caught in any real serious trouble. A new
chapter in my life began in July when I
rejoined the Air Force under my own name.

CHAPTER 6

SINNER OVERSEAS

CHAPTER 6

SINNER OVERSEAS

Life in the Air Force was made easier by my Army experience. For the first few months everything went along fine. I buckled down, determined to do a good job. Deep inside was the feeling of regret, a backlash of my actions in the Army.

At Keesler Air Base in Mississippi, I led the class in international Morse code. After 18 weeks of school, I was able to copy 30 words per minute, a faster rate than can be written by hand.

I was made class leader and joined a drill team. Thanks to my previous experience at close order drill and a strong urge to make a success at something, I became assistant drill instructor. When the instructor was transferred, I moved up in this place.

Life in the stockade, however unpleasant, had been good training. The guys respected my ability and fell right in line with my commands. One of the secrets of my success at this point was in having the men sing cadence instead of just saying it.

On the day the instructor first asked me to call cadence, I started singing and the musical beat made a hit with the group. Before long we were rated the best marching team on the base. As flight leader, I had charge of 240 men.

Through sheer determination and in my own strength, I was finally doing something worthwhile. But you can't remake an apple by putting on a new peel. Deep inside there was the subconscious knowledge that Paul McCulley was filled with all the old rottenness of human nature. The cancer of Sin was eating away at my soul while I put on a show for the men and myself.

Within the nine months I had earned two stripes. Somehow, I managed to survive a 30-day leave without getting into any serious trouble. I was still drinking, but the bottle, for the time being, apparently wasn't any bigger than I was.

Cross-training qualified me as an airborne radio operator before my assignment to a ground station. There was need, however, for an airborne radio man in the Philippine Islands. External social pressures which had been keeping me in line seemed to blow away on the winds of the South Pacific Islands.

I can't quite put my finger on it, but somehow the bottom seemed to fall out of everything. Rum and native drinks eliminated the veneer of self-respect. I couldn't remember what took place the night before as I suffered repeatedly through the mornings after.

I kissed goodbye to one stripe when I cussed out a Lieutenant Colonel flight commander. Soon after that an Air Police vehicle pulled alongside the motor scooter on which I was joy riding with two buddies. When the officer ordered me to stop I went faster and the attempted get away ended with the scooter running off the road. Next day I relinquished my other stripe.

During the year and a half that I served in the Philippines, I was arrested five times. Our five crews rotated in turn to Formosa (Taiwan) for one-week periods. The money setup made for a perfect black market operation. Regulations permitted us to change $200 from military script into "greenbacks." Personal habits prevented me from getting that much script on hand when it was my time to go. However, someone was always wanting a fellow to change a little extra for him.

Greenbacks could be taken to town and traded for pesos. The operation proved quite profitable when the pesos were exchanged for script. One black market operator paid cash for a new car and a house full of furniture when he returned to Wright Patterson Air Force Base in Ohio.

I traveled with this guy one time to Manila with close to $1,000 in greenbacks. You could nearly double your money with this kind of conduct. Most cash transactions were conducted in Angeles, which was much nearer our station than was Manila.

My base pay, before I lost my stripes, was $130 per month. Added to this was $55 per month for flying duty. I was always broke and borrowing money between paydays. When I walked through the pay line there was always a delegation waiting to get most of what I collected.

This monthly financial cycle should have said something to me had I been willing to face the fact of what was happening to me. Sin has its own system for borrowing before payday. The pleasures of doing wrong have their price. Payday's sure to come.

Just as sure as there is a settling-up day, sinners are met with a demand for settlement of their accounts.

CHAPTER 7

THE WAY DOWN

CHAPTER 7

THE WAY DOWN

About 150 people gathered at the airport to see me before my plane was to take off for the States again. Most of them were parents of the boys I had coached in a beginner's baseball team. The kids had responded really well to my leadership. For most of them it was the first time they had a glove in their hand. The Colonel had ended this activity due to my trouble-making excursions into town and because my drinking posed an unhealthy example for the Little Leaguers.

Life in the Philippines had its brighter moments in addition to the Little League. Even the base restriction tent provided its laughs.

As luck would have it, one of the first friends I made during my South Pacific stay was a Corporal named Charlie who wanted to learn international radio code. He proved to be a pretty good student and when the time came, the effort I had invested in teaching him netted very profitable returns.

I was placed in the restriction tent, along with about 10 other men, due to my drinking and trouble-making. Life seemed pretty dull at first. But then, with a flashlight, we attracted the attention of Charlie who was quartered close to our tent.

The signal code spelled out the message, "Bring us a case of beer and leave it near the tree." We later picked up the beer and left his money at the base of the tree, not far from the restriction tent. Our confinement area thereafter had the atmosphere of a semi-private bar. Following each party, we buried the evidence.

Life in the islands had given me one more chance to make the grade as a respectable human being; one of my best chances. But as usual I had blown it. However, the crowd assembled for my takeoff gave me a good feeling as they waved goodbye.

There was no need for airborne operators in the States since copilots and navigators could communicate on VHF frequencies. I had been cross-trained as a flight operations specialist at Wright Patterson Air Base in Dayton, Ohio. This was a vital skill since we were charged with keeping track of every aircraft entering or leaving our areas.

The lives of flight personnel and the safety of our nation's air defense aircraft were in our hands. Unfortunately, the bottle was all too frequently also in my hand. I really went heavy on the wine and before long I wasn't seeing too many sober days; often reporting for work drunk.

Airmen were startled one night to find me standing drunk at the gate stopping every car and asking their occupants for ID cards. Another time, I woke up in the service club. My shoes were off and blood was all over my arm and uniform. I had used my fist to smash a window to get into the club and sleep off another drunk.

Reports were getting back to the commanding officer. He had been told of the incident at the barracks when I broke windows in the door, challenged everyone to a fight, and punched a hole in the wall with my fists. To top it all off, I was often drunk enough to curse at other operators on the air and use foul language.

"The doctor wants to see you at the hospital," the commander said kindly when my conduct reports made some kind of action imperative. The doc turned out to be a psychologist, a rather nice guy who suggested I stay at the hospital awhile for observation. "Awhile" turned out to be six months in the alcoholic ward.

At the end of one month, I went on Antabuse, a drug developed to aid compulsive drinkers in shaking the habit.

They said I was a confirmed alcoholic, hiding behind the bottle. Antabuse makes a person sick when he drinks. They gave me a dose and then invited me to drink a can of beer. The results were disastrous.

When I recovered from this, they offered me a shot of wine. I became ill enough to never want to drink again.

But you can't transform a drunkard into a respectable citizen with a handful of pills. The problem is deeper than man and all his scientific genius can reach. I realized I needed help and was ready to be helped. Had the doctors and nurses known the answer, the following years of my life would have been different. But they didn't have the answer.

While in the hospital, I took the high school GED test and passed with excellent grades. At least I could go back to 8th and State with a diploma in my pocket.

I was released from the Air Force in July 1958, having served three years.

CHAPTER 8

INVITATION TO MURDER

CHAPTER 8

INVITATION TO MURDER

Not long after my release from the Air Force, I had a narrow escape with the law on a murder rap.

I had been drinking wine all day with a trio of friends. By evening I was so drunk I passed out on the steps of a house and the men left me there. A short time later, the three rolled a stranger and stomped him to death. Before they left the scene, they hid his body in some bushes. The only reason I wasn't in on the killing was that I had conked out on a cheap wine.

The cops nabbed Sam, one of the trio, later that night and locked him up for public drunkenness. In the jail was a third or fourth time loser, George, on his way to the Ohio state pen. George had stolen some watches and had broken parole. During their conversation, Sam told George about rolling the stranger. At this point Sam didn't know the robbery had resulted in death.

Early the following day, Larry Zwick went back to the scene of the murder and found the body still in the bushes where it had been left. Zwick went to the jail then to inform Sam of the stranger's death and to warn him to keep his mouth shut.

When Zwick and I were drinking and bumming around together later that afternoon, he told me he had something he needed my help on and asked me to meet him after dark. Suspecting the deal involved another robbery attempt, I was a little reluctant to agree. I told him I would meet him after he assured me, "It's nothing like that." At this point, I hadn't even heard of the murder.

Zwick's plan was that we would tie rocks on the body and drop it into Mill Creek. But even as we were talking, police were learning about the killing from George, who saw this as a way to detour his way around a prison term. George ignored Sam's request for silence and wrote a note to the prosecuting attorney offering to exchange his cooperation in solving a crime for leniency. It wasn't long before the cops had found the body and issued warrants for the three men involved. Zwick was in custody within an hour after asking for my help.

Zwick got 20 months in the pen after the jury found him guilty. He was the one who had done the kicking. Sam and Martin went to the pen also, with Martin doing the longest stretch, about three years, because of bad behavior.

Zwick had been given an early example which may have contributed to his criminal life. His Uncle John earned fame in the early 1930s by killing a policeman and being sentenced to life. When True Detective magazines ran the story, they publicized the killer's nickname, "The Fox."

Squealing paid off in George's case and he ended up serving only 30 days. In his defense, Zwick's attorney painted George as a modern-day Judas, drawing a parallel between the 30 pieces of silver for which Jesus was betrayed and the 30-days with which George got off for his deal.

Between the time of the murder and the trial an incident happened which increased our already strong hate for the police. It was about 1 p.m. and I was with a fellow waiting on the street corner for another friend. They were to play football and were headed to weigh in. A cop drove up and arrested us for loitering.

A newspaper story the following day stated that the cop had warned us all during the past two years to stay off the corner. I told the judge the cop was lying because I had been out of the Air Force just over a year. But the officer's story convinced the judge and we each got 30 days. Two of the fellows had their sentences suspended but Don Perkins and I had to serve time.

Headlines over the newspaper article had read "Court Aids Cleanup of Murder Area." We hated cops after that. Man, how we hated cops. If we had any respect for the law, it was all gone now.

We were beyond the power of any human being to change into reasonable men. The law was an enemy to be despised and resisted at every opportunity.

CHAPTER 9

ACCUSED OF RAPE

CHAPTER 9

ACCUSED OF RAPE

I, along with a few other fellows, were regular visitors to a restaurant on the lower floor of a favorite hangout near 8th and State. One of the fellows, a laborer for a pinball company, rented a couple of rooms on the third floor over the restaurant. It was a convenient place for us to idle away time and sleep.

One day, Tom, a fellow who had done time in Mansfield reformatory, asked if he could use one of the rooms. He told us he had a girl he wanted to take in there, so we let him use it.

He stuck his head out of the window a little while later and called to a few of us who were in a bunch just loafing on the street. He asked us to go down the street and get him a pint of wine. Tom dropped out 57 cents, which I used to make the purchase. I left the bottle by the door a few minutes later.

After a couple of hours went by and he hadn't come out, I got worried and went up there. I knocked on the door and yelled, "Open up." He answered "Later," and I told him, "Right now." The tone of my voice convinced him I meant business. A few seconds later the door flew open and he rushed by me and down the stairs.

I entered the room and found Karen, a 15-year-old girl, on the bed, blouse torn off and surrounded by blood and vomit. The room was a complete mess.

I gave her one of my shirts and got her some coffee to try and sober her up a little before taking her downstairs. The lady who ran the restaurant confronted me at the bottom of the stairs and started accusing me of rape. Her charges included having a number of other women up there and having at times pimped for them.

"Now you've taken that girl up there and raped her," she said. Tom, who was on probation at the time, was scared to death of criminal charges and tried to make it look as if I had done it.

Tom just stood there with the women. Karen was afraid of Tom's girlfriend, a huge woman who later became his wife. Confronted with the bigger female, Karen wouldn't tell the truth of what had happened. She said she couldn't remember who had attacked her, but thought it might have been me.

Circumstantial evidence, along with Karen's story, was enough to convict me in the eyes of the 8th and State neighborhood. This hung over my head until about two weeks later when I called Karen on the telephone and had one of the girls in the neighborhood get on the extension phone to listen. Karen told me over the wire that she realized it was Tom who had committed the rape, but fear of Barbara prevented her from telling the truth.

That was enough to clear me of the crime as far as the kids around the neighborhood were concerned. There were no formal charges made against anyone.

Karen's life from that point, according to street talk, descended from bad to worse. Stories made the rounds telling how she had begun running with some of the most despised men of the area.

Everyone around 8th and State, of course, had a bad reputation to some extent. The address alone marked a person as something less than a decent citizen. But some had much worse reputations than others. Karen's conduct marked her as a woman of the lowest kind.

For people with a cause—a reason for living—life holds a series of adventures. Life in a big city for those who have no purpose lacks this thrill-of-living element. Sex, along with alcohol and dope, offers a synthetic kind of joy.

The existence of a sinner is a phony copy of real life. Some things seen attractive—viewing them from the outside for the first time or two. But the city is man-made, reflecting in most every aspect the complete deprivation of natural man's spirit. City streets and buildings form a sort of concrete prison for those already imprisoned in mind and soul.

Sex, to the lost, is a drug promising pleasure but delivering along with it a sickening dish of human misery. Karen, as she lay unconscious on the bed that day, almost perfectly reflected the image of all sexual indulgence outside of marriage.

CHAPTER 10

BASEBALL AND STOLEN CARS

CHAPTER 10

BASEBALL AND STOLEN CARS

Things had changed quite a bit when I got back to 8th and State in the summer of 1958 following my Air Force hitch. Most of the fellows were gone and a younger crowd had taken over. Baseball was still a favorite pastime and ability to perform on the diamond could make a guy pretty popular.

When I wasn't hitting the bottle, or bumming in the streets, I was playing ball. Quite often we were involved in beer games. These contests ended with the losing team buying a barrel of beer for the winners. More often than not, a second barrel was purchased and both sides ended up with plenty to drink.

During the summer of 1959, I played on a team with a pretty good player named Pete Rose. I also coached a girls' softball team which included Pete's sister, Carol. Carol didn't seem to have inherited much of Pete's aptitude for the sport, but she had a nice personality.

One of my drinking partners was a fellow we called Doc, a married man with two grown children. One day I borrowed his car to pick up my girlfriend and drive her home after work. I returned the vehicle to him and we separated about 9 p.m. after drinking together. I went back later and took his car without telling him. Then I began making the rounds in different sections of town.

It must have been about 10 a.m. the next morning when I woke up in Cincinnati General Hospital, strapped to the bed and completely naked. A doctor was in the room and a police officer was standing over me. "Ah, shut up. You've been complaining ever since you've been here. This is a heck of a time to be modest," the doctor said when I asked to be covered. I had no idea what had happened. "You had a car wreck," the cop explained. This didn't tell me much. I thought I must have killed someone.

"Well, whose car was it?" I asked.

"Why I don't know, don't you know?" he questioned.

"I don't remember nothing," I told him. It's an awful feeling to wake up in the hospital with a broken jaw, your leg busted and your ankles shackled together; a policeman sitting at the foot of your bed. He stayed there three days, until Doc and Mary discovered it was I who had taken the car. They dropped the charge of auto theft.

I was in the hospital nine days, fortunate to be alive. My head had gone through the windshield giving me a fractured jaw and lacerations of the head. Forty stitches had been required to close the wound in my left kneecap area. This part of my body had smashed through the dashboard and been torn by the metal.

Somebody had put up my bond, and I was given a date to appear in court on charges of driving under suspension, destruction of city property, conversion and a number of other violations. A friend of mine called a friend of his who was a friend of the judge, and when I went to court I got $10 and costs twice. Charges had been reduced to driving with no license and reckless driving.

Having gotten out of this mess with comparative ease, I became a porter in a couple of the bars. I would sweep the floors in return for what the managers would let me drink before the customers arrived. I would say, "Hey, Eddie, you want me to sweep the floor?" He'd say yes and I'd start sweeping and drinking.

Even with the braces on my teeth and my jaws clamped together, I stayed drunk for nine weeks. I couldn't eat, but I could drink. Luckily, I didn't vomit pure blood. It would stream out of my mouth and nose, then I'd just go back to the bar and start drinking again.

My dad died shortly after the time of my accident. About four or five months later my brother died, at age 36, with five children who would remember him as a heavy drinker.

This latest brush with my own eternity and the departure of two loved ones should have brought me to my senses. But I wasn't quite ready to seek a way out of my existence of sin and suffering. It was now August 1963 and my final arrest for drunkenness was still a month away.

CHAPTER 11

KNEADING DOUGH

CHAPTER 11

KNEADING DOUGH

There is always a way when the price is needed for a bottle. To sinners in the city, the opportunity to steal and rob was an ever-present temptation.

Zwick had possession of the key to a bakery where he had had been employed. One night as we were out bumming around in a car he had borrowed from a friend of his, we decided we needed money. We had been drinking and exhausted our resources.

We let ourselves in the front door of the bakery, knocked the lock off the drawer on one side of a desk and got about $10 in change. After another two hours of drinking, we were broke again. "Hey," Zwick ventured, "I know where there are some greenbacks." A short time later we were back inside of the bakery busting the lock on the other side of the desk.

The take on this second visit netted us $34 in greenbacks. We stayed out all night bumming around, ending up the next morning in a popular restaurant hangout where the talk centered pretty much around the robbery. The bakery was located about half a block from the police station and the cops were apparently embarrassed by the crime—twice in one night—right under their noses.

I was never even questioned in connection with the robbery. A favorite trick of ours was to take the last bus at night into the suburbs and steal anything with which we could turn a fast buck. Cameras, watches, radios—anything was fair game—if it could be offered to buyers on the street the next day. Sometimes our merchandise was exchange for a pawn ticket, but most of it was sold directly to those who preferred to purchase with a minimum of questions.

Three of us boarded the last bus going through 8th and State for the Bond Hill section. This was a nice well-to-do neighborhood. When we arrived, we started going through automobiles and garages. It must have been about 2 a.m. when a party was in progress upstairs at one house. We were cutting through backyards when we came on the scene, finding the garage doors wide open. As we entered the garage, one of the boys just reached up and turned the light on. The party went on without interruption as we did our dirty work. The only thing of value was a radio.

The next place we hit was a house with a detached garage made for three or four vehicles. Our flashlight shined on a leather pouch on the rear seat of a brand-new automobile. When attempts to unlock the doors with wire lifters failed, one of the boys smashed a window with a brick. His arm became stuck in the hole and we had a hard time freeing it without his flesh being cut on the jagged edges.

Meanwhile, dogs were barking all over the neighborhood and lights were coming on in the houses. We snatched the pouch and took off running. Our flight ended a few minutes later behind some bushes on a golf course where we eagerly tore into the expensive leather container. We found only some insurance papers. Our victim was a salesman.

One time we parked a hot car right next to the place where a fellow was staying who had just been released from the Ohio Penitentiary. We wanted to make sure he got the blame for it. The police took him for questioning, but they later freed him.

We robbed a lot of homes on our last bus excursion into the surrounding areas. Stolen items sold for about $3.00 to $5.00 each on the street and we used the money for drinking and bennies. One of the fellows was on paregoric.

CHAPTER 12

PINBALL MACHINES WERE "IN"

CHAPTER 12

PINBALL MACHINES WERE "IN"

Gambling on the pinball machines was the "in" thing in Cincinnati and Northern Kentucky during the 1950s. Although it was against the law, everybody seemed to be doing it and the police just turned their heads.

It was New Year's Eve, 1954, when I first saw a professional "driller" in action at a small restaurant. I had only two dollars to my name when I got change and put in the first of my nickels. I won four games on the first coin; pushed two games and had two showing on the register when the professional walked over. This guy had the style and lingo of a con man.

As he stood around the right side of the back of the machine, the sharpie seemed casually interested in my game. When I glanced up at the back board, I had 33 registered instead of two. "If you want me to go on, we'll split it three ways, between me, you, and my broad." I took a second gander at the games registered and told him, "You know what you're doing man. Go ahead."

I hit four in a row, which should have given me 70 games, but he ran it smoothly to 250. He then tilted the machine so the odds wouldn't show and I called the waitress for the payoff.

It was a slick operation all the way. The guy must have spent some time in the pen. He had expert knowledge of machines and the use of electric drills. Anyone who was anybody in this section of town was either in the pen, recently released or headed for prison. He had come into the joint with this girlfriend, a buxom blond, rough looking and wearing a skirt and red sweater. She sat at the counter with her legs crossed; a good spot to center attention away from her partner's activity.

After the payoff, we moved out on the street where he said, "Give me $7.50. Keep the rest for yourself." He then offered to let me make the rounds with him, splitting the take from other machines. I would have gone with the guy, but a friend came along about that time, half drunk, and I went with him instead.

The con man was really slick. We later figured he used a miniature electric drill to get through the back of the machine and run up the odds with a fine wire. But we searched the back boards in vain looking for the hole.

Beating the pinball machines by drilling became popular among the hoods of the neighborhood, but we never developed the professional touch. We managed to make enough to live it up a little by using a corkscrew.

We drilled machines in the poolroom and in about 13 bars, taking small amounts from each before branching out into other neighborhoods. There were two types of machines. On the "bingo" variety you played to get your numbers in a row. On the "horserace" style, you could get $100 after working up the odds.

One time five or six of us walked into a bar with only one dollar among us. We crowded around a machine to keep other customers from seeing what we were up to. While one played, another used the corkscrew. But before we got the hole finished, we used up our last nickel. It was all set for us to use a wire through the hole and up the odds by tripping the game mechanism. When we went back the next day and started walking toward the back of the bar where the machine sat, some guy called out "there's the boys that drilled your pinball machine." We took off in a hurry.

Machine owners couldn't complain to police when they were cheated since they were involved in an illegal operation themselves. When things got too rough for them they took matters in their own hands.

After they beat up a professional driller in wide-open Newport, the message got around pretty fast that the same treatment was in store for anyone else who took the big boys for too much. They converted the machine not too long after that with steel backs that couldn't be drilled.

Photo right: That's me in the cap when I was 15 years old with Bill "Skeeter" Cassidy, age 18.

Photo below: They said I was whistling at a girl. I'm 18 years old. That's Lee, my brother, on the right. This was taken at the Western Plaza in Cincinnati.

Below: 8th and State Street, Cincinnati, Ohio, in 2017.

CHAPTER 13

WORKHOUSE BLUES

CHAPTER 13

WORKHOUSE BLUES

Existence, you could hardly call it living, in the Cincinnati workhouse was beyond the imagination of many people.

About 600 prisoners were kept there each day. While they were serving sentences for minor crimes, they were often prisoners with a long history of serious or violent crimes. One fellow I met in there had done 20 years on a murder rap.

There were men from all over the country and they all agreed that the Cincinnati workhouse was the worst they had ever seen. Guards locked you in your cell with a key each night and unlock it again in the morning. Individual cells had no plumbing and the only facilities were an iron bed, straw mattress and blanket, a pillow without a case, and a bucket.

About two inches of disinfectant was used in the bottom of each bucket. The odor was almost unbearable as some 600 men formed into two lines to empty their buckets into the cesspool. A worker used a coffee can to dip fresh disinfectant into the buckets from a 55-gallon drum.

The breakfast lines formed right past the cesspool and the hungry prisoners were required to sit down, one table at a time, upon the command of a guard. No talking was permitted. If you wanted salt, the only thing on the table, you rapped on the table, the signal for someone to pass it along.

Cells were arranged in blocks with about 30 to 40 on each deck. Decks were made up on ranges, such as C, D, E and F. On range C there were about five or six tiers, each containing about 35 cells.

Men with six months or less were given work details, a welcome release from the inactivity of the cells. Those who were not working had little else to do except play dominos. Prisoners were so keyed up that fights over little things were common. I have seen grown men get into knock-down, drag-out fights over a candy bar.

Work details gave us contact with the outside. City vehicles were brought in to be washed, providing a chance for friends to bring in food and other items from the outside. Sometimes, we even sent out for restaurant food.

Details were formed for the washing of police vehicles at the various stations. These gave opportunity for men to obtain wine along with food items. It was not uncommon to see men half drunk in the workhouse.

Sexual perversion of new, young prisoners was the accepted thing. A first timer, unless he was lucky enough to have friends on the inside, was almost always forced into perverted acts.

Fortunately for me, the 8th and State neighborhood was always well represented in the workhouse. Thus, I was always well represented in the workhouse. I was spared the common fate of newcomers when I pulled my first workhouse stretch at the age of 20.

Like prisoners anywhere, the inmates hated guys who would rat on them for infractions of the rules. One guy, Robert the Rat, almost lost his life because he squealed on the men. Every time he learned about someone having contraband he would go to prison officials and tell them what was going on.

Word spread around the workhouse one day that it was time to put an end to his ratting. A large group of prisoners formed and began walking toward Robert. As he backed away, he realized that they intended to kill him. Someone dropped a large bucket from a walkway several cells above and it just missed the backward-walking rat. Then someone else dropped a cup which glanced off his shoulder.

He took off running, failing to stop at the white line which formed the boundary between the men and their guards. He yelled at the top of his voice, "Let me out of here, they are going to kill me." The guard turned his back, seemingly indifferent to his plight as the mob closed in. Then, as they almost reached him, the guards opened the gate and let him out.

We didn't see him after that. They no doubt put him in the hospital or in another special part of the workhouse for the remainder of his sentence. Had we been able to get our hands on him he wouldn't have stood a chance.

In spite of the animal-like atmosphere, a large number of men sought to be confined to the workhouse. I remember one man, who was sentenced to six months, asking the judge, "Can't you make it a year, your Honor?"

There may have been good reasons for the deplorable state within the workhouse walls. Had things been any better, there might have been twice the number of men "applying" for admission.

CHAPTER 14

TURNING POINT

CHAPTER 14

TURNING POINT

The wonder of the ages is the fact that God loves sinful men and will reach into the filth of human existence to reach the vilest wretch. Unknown to me, he had arranged for me to meet him on my seventh stretch in the workhouse.

Following a night of sin, I woke up in a jail cell and the frightening experience with that giant cockroach. As that horrible insect crawled toward me, the indescribable fear I knew was only one of many experiences that helped in causing me to begin coming to myself

The Bible, in telling the story of a wayward son, says, "He came to himself." This is what was happening to me, Paul McCulley, as I waited in line for the judge to hand me another 10-day sentence and as I rode in the paddy wagon toward the workhouse.

I was sick—sick of drinking, sick of robbing, cheating and hurting everyone around me. I had been in the gutter and behind bars long enough. The weight of years of sinning pressed down on my being and I wanted something, anything, that would get me out of the pig pen of sin.

AA offers a program for people who are enslaved by the bottle. I volunteered for it as soon as I reached the workhouse. The coordinator questioned me sincerely when I talked to him about it. On a previous sentence I had volunteered for the program, interested only in the special privileges it afforded the men. Something in the tone of my voice told the coordinator that I meant business this time.

The program, as far as it goes, is a good one. Men are freed from the humiliating routine of the slop bucket lines, the food is better, and there are even television privileges up until 10:00 p.m. AA gives special education concerning such things as the effect of alcohol on the mind and body. The only thing wrong with the program is that it doesn't go far enough.

Alcoholics claim there is no cure for their sickness. But thank God, I know different. Christ Jesus came into the world to save sinners and his power can overcome anything. Those who claim the bottle can't be defeated know nothing of the power of God.

In the prison library I was led to a book, First Questions on the Life of the Spirit. I thought it was a ghost story and I wanted something spooky to take back to my bunk and read. As I lay there the Spirit began getting a hold on me. The words just jumped out at me.

The author said that at one time he hadn't known a thing about God. I thought, "That's me. I don't know a thing about God or Christianity." But he mentioned something that helped him and I decided to try it. He said that if a man will keep repeating a word over and over to himself he will just naturally want to make the effort to find out something about it.

I began saying over and over in my mind, "God, God, God, God," and soon began searching to learn about Him. I turned to the Bible, even though it seemed to make little sense to me.

After my release from the workhouse, I continued for a few weeks in the AA program. I enjoyed the program and appreciated the efforts of the fellows in AA to help me. But I needed something more.

During many of my previous drunks, I had become acquainted with a friend as she went on her way to a little Methodist Church on Sunday mornings. She was always friendly and would say hi to me. When I felt a need to go to church and was ashamed to be by myself, I called her up and asked her if she would sit by me if I was going to attend. She said, "Sure."

I couldn't understand most of what was going on. I was so spiritually dead that I couldn't understand even the simplest Scripture teachings. Rev. Carter, the pastor, was a wonderful Christian man and he did his best to help and encourage me. He invited me to prayer meetings and I joined a membership class.

Many of the church members showed an interest in me. But I wasn't ready to join the church. I was all dirty inside, filthy without anything to commend me to either man or God. There is a familiar song, "Just as I Am," that has been heard many times and I found out later that is how God accepts us. Just as we are. Quitting bad habits cannot save a man. A man must realize he is a sinner, confess his sins, and by faith accept Christ as his Savior. It took me quite a while to learn this.

CHAPTER 15

AMAZING GRACE

CHAPTER 15

AMAZING GRACE

For ten nights I prayed, seeming unable to reach God. My life was so soaked in the filthy sewers of sin that I couldn't even be sorry for what I had done. I had to pray "God, help me to be sorry for what I have done."

I had robbed, cheated and stolen. I had broken the law at every opportunity. I was rotten to the core.

One of the conditions of membership in the Methodist Church was that you pledged to do or not to do certain things. So, on the night of the final membership class, I started on my way to tell Rev. Carter about it. I had thought out what I was going to say, "Reverend Carter, I cannot join your church. One of the conditions is that a member pray for the church. I can't pray; I don't know how. Another condition is that a person support the church with his money. How can I do that? I don't work. Then a person has to promise to attend the services. I can't do that. I might be in the workhouse again before next Sunday!"

On the way to the membership class, I stopped in a small restaurant and had a soft drink as I resigned myself to the idea that I would have to spend the rest of my life in the pigpen and go to Hell. There was no hope for me.

I walked out of the restaurant and started to cross the intersection of 8th and State when it happened! A miracle took place right there as I was in the middle of 8th and State! God flooded my being with light. The warmest feeling came over me. I didn't know what had happened, but sensed that the great burden of guilt was gone from my back.

I ran all the way from that corner to the church. I told him, "Rev. Carter, I'll join your church. I'm ready, I know I've been saved."

The light and love that filled me that instant in the middle of 8th and State has never let up. The Bible says, "If any man be in Christ, he is a new creature." Paul McCulley was a new creature, born again by the Spirit. I had left the muddy slop of sin and been given citizenship in Heaven with my Father.

No longer was that compulsion of sin to control my personality. Life had replaced death and the prodigal had come home.

The Lord was working on those around me, also. Rev. Carter held an invitation at the close of Sunday's service. I held back from that public confession, but on the last verse of the final hymn I went to the altar. Some of the members knelt in silent prayer.

My first thought was Al, my best buddy. He just had to know what Christ had done for me and more than anything else I wanted him and Doris, his wife, to be saved.

They didn't understand it and thought I was crazy when I told them what had happened. After I left their house, they talked it over wondering what my angle was. "I wonder what he's up to this time," Doris asked. They came to watch my baptism, thinking I must have gone off my rocker somehow.

All things are new to the Christian, and it wasn't long before Al and Doris knew that a real change had taken place in my life. Al began to want what I had and before long I possessed the unexplainable joy of leading my best friend to my Savior. Doris accepted the gospel, too, and before long their home, once a scene of drinking and fighting, became a center of love and affection.

Not everyone accepted or understood the complete change that had taken place in me.

Various estimates were made as to the length of time I would "hold out." When God does something, it is done right.

I grew stronger in the faith. I got a job and began to give more than my tithe to the church. God blessed at every turn. I soon learned one of the basic truths of Christian living; you can't outgive God.

Life was exciting now. God had reached down to the intersection of 8th and State and rescued a Hell-bound sinner. I couldn't keep quiet! I had to tell everyone the good news.

It wasn't long before I knew God was calling me to preach.

CHAPTER 16

THE LIBERAL DENOMINATION

CHAPTER 16

THE LIBERAL DENOMINATION

It was difficult at first for me to even say the Lord's name in a decent way. I was so used to saying it as a curse word that it was a strange experience when I first began to try to utter it in prayer.

When I finally got God's name out and started praying, I began trying to bargain with Him. "Lord, if you will do this, I'll do that." Then the Spirit was striving with me and I finally realized I needed to confess.

As I began to grow in the things of God after my conversion, His grace was increased in my life. A few months following the miracle of my new birth, I entered business college and started to study accounting along with some programming. Then, a door opened for me to go to work with Holiday Inn.

I obtained this job through an employment agency because of my record. I had gone to several places and applied for work, but they turned me away because of my record. "You are just a bum." "Get out of here." "Do you think we are crazy enough to hire a man with 30 arrests on his record?"

God's new creature was in His hands. My starting salary was $250 per month for six days per week. After one year as a desk clerk and assistant innkeeper, I left the company to preach full time. That same week they asked me to take over as innkeeper, but I quit instead, as I felt God leading this way in my life.

I went to Jackson, Ohio, as a minister for three congregations in one of the mainline denominations. My wife also quit her $100 per week job as a secretary and we went into the work on a promise of only $75 per week. The money was not important to us. We wanted only to obey God and win men and women for His Kingdom. We were given a house, but were required to pay all the utilities and furnish gas for our car. We were with this big denomination for six months.

We held revival meetings at our Winchester, Ohio, congregation. One lady told us this was the first time in 25 years that the church building had been filled with people. Folks were saved and brought to a closer walk with God.

Lacking formal training, I didn't know this simple preaching of the Word was no longer practiced by most churches in this liberal denomination.

During a revival series in which each night a different preacher was given a turn to speak before the message, I got up and asked for testimonies. I noticed the pastor and evangelist look at each other as they sat on the platform. While the other ministers had read their prayer, I just spoke to God from the heart.

The evangelist met me at the door and at the close of the service the following night, an ugly scene was created as he objected to my zeal.

My eyes were opened further at a ministers' conference. One veteran preacher put a chair in the center of the room, sat on it and asked, "Who believes in being converted?" One man stood up and said, "I've been preaching for 27 years and I don't believe in conversion. The Bible says we are all sinners. If we are all sinners, why be converted? The Bible says that Christ died for the sinner."

I was quickly on my feet. "Do you mean you are trying to tell me there is nothing to being converted?" It was hard for me to believe this was taking place in a denomination which once preached the pure gospel.

"I thank God," I told him, "that two years ago, while I was stumbling around the streets of Cincinnati—a drunken bum—that while I was searching for help, He didn't lead me to your church. I needed to hear something about being converted."

To support his argument, he quoted 1 John 1:8, "If we say we have no sin we deceive ourselves and the truth is not in us." At that time, I didn't know the next verse, which would have been the perfect answer to this unconverted minister.

"If we confess our sins, He is faithful and just to forgive us our sins, and to cleanse us from all unrighteousness" (9).

The God who reached down to rescue me from sin was about to rescue again—this time from ministers who did not understand the words of Jesus when He said, "You must be born again."

CHAPTER 17

OUT AND ON WITH GOD

CHAPTER 17

OUT AND ON WITH GOD

The ministers conference had ended. Six or seven of the fellows believed in being born again. The rest of them were preaching something else. The liberal ministers shied away from me like I had the plague. In their eyes, I was a fanatic, an odd ball.

In contrast to their actions, those who knew what it means to be converted gathered around me to advise "Son, you just keep on preaching it the way you see it. Don't you be taken in by this modern stuff."

With all this happening, I observed that many ministers were more interested in membership and money than they were in the souls of men. We had a quota that we had to get in church membership every year. Papers from denominational headquarters sent out quotas for money. They never mentioned a burden for people or winning the lost.

The district superintendent sent for me and I went to see him. He said, "This conversion that you had is a miracle. What happened to you just doesn't happen, except about once every thousand years." I answered, "Why? If you are a Christian, you have been converted." He replied, "Oh, no, I have always been raised in the church. I never had anything like you are talking about." I told him, "Then you probably are not a Christian."

With this he exploded, "I know you guys. You're a dime a dozen." The meeting ended with some remark about my stupidity and I left. On Sunday, I reported to my churches all that had been said. A letter arrived for me on Monday from the district superintendent asking me to reconsider my stand.

During this time, I was preaching a revival at a nearby city. The district coordinator paid me a visit. He was the type of guy who reads every word of his sermon and prescribed prayers.

He came into the parsonage, never looking me in the eye, and sat there telling me I had to "quit preaching against the denomination." Because I had taken a stand in opposition to sin in the church and hypocrisy, they had taken it for granted that I was preaching against the organized church.

He noted, "We have had some reports that you have been throwing stones at our denomination. We want you to stay here as the pastor of this church; the people want you, too. You are going to have to quit preaching against our denomination as you are. You are striking out against the church."

I just got up and went to the door, opened it and informed him, "You can leave now. I want you to know that you didn't call me to preach. You can tell the district superintendent that he hasn't called me to preach. God called me to preach and I'll preach whatever He lays on my heart."

"Well, get your furniture and get out of this parsonage, and quit preaching the revival. We are cutting you off from there, too."

The pastor at the church where the services were being held was also ready to come out of the modernistic denomination. About 35 of the people got together and sent a spokesman to me asking me to continue with the meetings.

My wife went to stay with my old buddy, Al, and his wife. We put our furniture in storage. The church folks rented a house for me and we continued our services in an old beer joint. We moved in a piano and chairs and preached the Word. Many were saved as God blessed in answer to prayer.

Following the revival, I went back to work for the Holiday Inn and began attending the First Church of God at Evendale. For three years, under the preaching of Brother Ralph Turner, the Word cut deeply into my being, cutting away the pride.

I began to be molded by the Lord into a useful member of His army.

CHAPTER 18

CALLED TO RICHMOND

CHAPTER 18

CALLED TO RICHMOND

Countless blessings came into my life while I attended the Evendale First Church of God and went to seminary.

The Holy Spirit led me into a deeper experience of grace. My secure work provided many opportunities to lead men to Christ. My foreman on one job was backslidden and had once been a Baptist preacher. The Lord spoke to him as we talked and prayed. Before long, this former preacher was bringing his Bible to work and together we shared the Good News with fellow workers.

While I was preaching at various churches, I would often look out and see men with whom I had worked during the day. They observed in my experience something they wanted and when it was time to pray, a lot of them raised their hands.

Souls were being saved and we rejoiced at God's work among the spiritually hungry.

The Devil was constantly fighting against the Word of the Lord, but we say demonstrated time and time again, "greater is He that is in you than he that is in the world."

The hand of God was opening another door of service at Richmond, Kentucky. I preached in Richmond's First Church of God in June 1969 and November of that year I became the pastor of that congregation.

The Lord blessed constantly as we attempted to share His truths with souls within and without the church. His Holy Spirit began working among the church people, showing us His great plan for reaching the lost. Various Christians came to a realization that God wanted them on the move.

We found a fruitful ministry in the hospital, jail, and in the homes of the people of Madison County. A very evident need existed everywhere and the Holy Spirit touched lives through a daily broadcast which we called "Pathways to God." For fifteen minutes each day, five days per week, we told the glorious news that Christ Jesus came into the world to seek and to save sinners.

Soon we were giving a new tool with which to tell what God can do for lost humanity. Madison County was given a weekly newspaper which sought to give fair coverage to all news.

An employee of the Madison County Newsweek was driving along the street near the parsonage one day when his auto quit running. He knocked on the door and asked to use the phone to call a service station. While waiting for someone to come and fix the car, we entered into a discussion about the Lord.

No cause was ever found for that auto ceasing to run that day. The mechanic examined it and said, "There is nothing wrong with it." God had allowed the mechanical failure and revealed His reason a few days later, after we had prayed about it.

In the newspaper office the reporter agreed to write the story, just as it had happened and to tell it in the series "Sinnerman." Through the publication of this story in serial form, considerable interest was generated in the power of the Gospel to redeem lives.

All the glory belongs to God. It took a miracle to change the sinnerman from 8th and State into a minister of the Gospel. God stands always ready to perform this same miracle in the life of anyone who will permit him to do so.

CHAPTER 19

DEALING WITH DIFFICULTIES

CHAPTER 19

DEALING WITH DIFFICULTIES

Accepting Christ is the beginning of a new, happy, exciting life. However, the Christian experience is a growth process. As a newborn baby grows, crawls, stands, walks, and eventually runs, so it is in the Spiritual realm.

Growth is painful. Why? We grow through trial and difficulties. Growth comes when we learn to trust God through our adversities.

We sometimes believe that when we become a Christian, life will be easy, a "bed of roses." Not so! The old saying "no pain, no gain" applies to the Christian life as well. The difference? Christ is with the Christian! Remember, Jesus said, "Come unto me all ye that labor and are heavy laden and I will give you rest."

He also said, "Take my yoke upon you and learn of me." In facing life's problems, the Christian has the advantage of the Word of God, the Power of the Holy Spirit, and the promise that Jesus made of never leaving or forsaking us.

The thrill of Christianity is knowing that Christ is with us. God specializes in the impossible. He turns despair into hope; hate into love. Every Christian can look back with "20/20 hindsight" and see clearly that God has always been there.

Jesus said, "The thief cometh not but to steal, kill, and destroy. But I've come that ye may have life and have it more abundantly." The Apostle Paul talked about our cups being full and running over. He also stated, "I can do all things through Christ which strengtheneth me." The Apostle Peter wrote of the "joy unspeakable and full of glory."

There are hundreds of promises in the Bible encouraging the followers of Christ. But at the same time there are Scriptures that teach us of crosses to bear and opposition from the "enemy of our soul." As a matter of fact, when our faith is strong, we as Christians can view problems as opportunities.

Just as in Ezekiel's vision of the valley of the dry bones, where God reveals that the Word of God and the Holy Spirit work together, it was the preaching of the prophet that brought the bones together, but the wind (Holy Spirit) brought life to the dry bones.

The power of the Word and the Holy Spirit in our lives teaches us to say with the Apostle Paul, "We are more than conquerors through Christ." Before Christ came into my life I thought that all Christians were perfect and protected by an invisible shield, "but all of my failures are teaching me that God loves me and cares not only for my eternal life, but for my present life."

Just as Jesus had a cross to bear, so does every Christian. But God has promised that if we draw close to Him, He will draw close to us.

In the 8th and State intersection, I had a dramatic spiritual experience. I felt that surge of the loving and forgiving power of God. For months I lived in a spiritual "bubble." It seemed as if I were impervious to anything "of the world!" Then God burst the bubble!

I started to realize that I was only a babe in Christ. I had to learn how to crawl. Many times, as in the life of Job, God uses the negative to teach us the positives.

CHAPTER 20

A CONTINUING SUPPORT SYSTEM

CHAPTER 20

A CONTINUING SUPPORT SYSTEM

In the parable of the Good Samaritan, Jesus told of the man who was attacked by robbers, left for dead by the religious leaders, and cared for by a foreigner. To my way of looking at it, he was beaten up by the world, passed up by the church, and picked up by Christ.

In his "farewell address," Jesus told His disciples that it was necessary for Him to return to Heaven or the Comforter would not come. He was speaking of the Holy Spirit.

Isn't it good to know that God the Father, Jesus his Son, and the Holy Spirit provides us with a "divine support system!"

As with the man in the parable, we can be "beaten up by the world." Jesus was "in the right," but He was beaten up by the world. Have you ever lost your job unfairly? Have your friends ever forsaken you? Have you ever been disappointed by a family member?

All of us have had bad experiences that have caused us to say, "Why me, Lord?"

Thank God for the Divine Connections!

God does not call us into His family to give us a name and let us fend for ourselves. There is a "Connection" between the Heavenly Father and all of His children. For an example: In Paul's letter to Rome he wrote, "All things that were written before times were written for our learning. That we through patience and comfort of the Scriptures might have hope."

That tells us that the Bible was written for our learning and to give us hope. There are many other Scriptures that relate to the Word of God as a "Divine Connection" between the Creator and the created.

Visit any bookstore and you will see shelf after shelf of "self-help" books. But God gave us the greatest self-help book of all when He gave us the Bible!

The Holy Spirit is also a "Divine Connection." The Apostle John wrote, quoting Jesus, "Howbeit when he the Spirit of truth is come, he will guide you into all truth." He also said, "It is expedient for you that I go away; for if I go not away the Comforter will not come unto you; but if I depart, I will send him unto you."

Jesus said that the Holy Ghost will teach you what to say. In the Old Testament, Nehemiah wrote, "God gave the good Spirit to instruct them." The Bible promises that the Spirit of God will live in us.

It is difficult to explain how the Holy Spirit works in the lives of God's children; it's just as difficult as trying to explain electricity! But it works!

Remember my near-fatal automobile accident? I believe that the "Divine Connection" and intervention of the Holy Spirit is very personal and very close.

As we grow, by faith in God, we can sense His nearness constantly, performing miracles and urging the Christian to a victorious life.

Another link in the Divine Connection is prayer.

CHAPTER 21

THE PRAYER CONNECTION

CHAPTER 21

THE PRAYER CONNECTION

There's so much to say about prayer! What is prayer? How is one supposed to pray? Prayer is simply "communication with God." It is a two-way connection. Prayer is not only telling God our needs, but also listening for Him to direct us.

How is one supposed to pray? When the disciples asked Jesus to teach them to pray, He gave to them what we now call the "The Lord's Prayer" (Luke 11:2-4). The design of the Lord's Prayer is a guide for us to address God.

Our conversation with God must be truthful and direct. We can't lie to God anyway! Share with Him as you would with a trusted friend or counselor. You can tell Him your deepest secrets.

My first attempt at prayer was a disaster! I couldn't even say God's name aloud. It seemed as though my mind blocked my heart from uttering God's name. But I was determined to break through that barrier. I was wrestling with myself, and I knew the positive side had to win.

Victory came after days of simply saying, "God, help me to be sorry for what I have done." As I reflect on that time, I know that God was trying to speak to me. But my spiritual ears were closed.

I began to repent after I was to utter that simple plea, "God, help me to be sorry." At that time, I faintly heard the voice of God. It wasn't until the 8th and State miracle that I experienced the forgiving and loving power of God.

Now I had met a friend I could talk to. Someone who would listen and care! All prayers are answered either "yes", "no", or "wait awhile." Shortly after I was saved, I prayed for "things." Some of them I received, some not.

I remember one occasion when I told God if a certain incident didn't happen, I didn't know if I could live. I thanked God for saying, "No!" How blessed we are that God always knows what is best for us.

God created us for fellowship with Him. Prayer is the most vital connecting link in that fellowship. The Bible encourages us to pray. Jesus urged us to pray. You can pray kneeling, standing, reclining, thinking silently, or out loud. Anytime, anyplace.

The "lines" to God remain open—no busy signals! He wants to hear from you! He wants to hear your problems, dreams, hopes, successes, and failures. Prayer is powerful. It can move mountains and change lives.

God can change in an instant what man in his intelligence struggles with for years. My "fifteen minutes a day" formula will change your life forever:

1. Five minutes of reading your Bible.
2. Five minutes of talking to God. (communication transmitted)
3. Five minutes of listening to God. (communication received)

Think of this as your daily "spiritual exercise." I found it easy to read and talk, but somewhat difficult to listen. Doing my spiritual exercises taught me that what God had to say to me was more important than what I had to say to Him!

Do I hear a "voice" speaking to me? No! The spiritual exercises will enable you to develop "spiritual ears" and you will hear that "still, small voice." And you will know it's God talking to you.

I am so thankful for the day God heard my prayer.

A drunken, hopeless, useless bum rose from the vile filth of a big city neighborhood, to become a preacher of the gospel. "God sent not His Son into the World to condemn the World; but that the world through Him might be saved."

You, too, can know Jesus as your personal Savior. No matter how far in sin you have gone, even if you feel as though you haven't a friend in the world, I want you to know that Jesus loves you. What He has done for me, He can do for you.

Accept Him now.

ABOUT THE AUTHOR

Paul McCulley still lives in the Cincinnati area. After preaching for more than 30 years, he served as Ohio's representative to Washington DC when "faith-based initiatives" were being coordinated by President George Bush. Paul worked with Congressman Rob Portman (pictured below). Paul still serves as interim pastor for churches and chaplain for the Clermont Co., Ohio, Corrections Facility. He is married and has three grown children.

Be sure to order extra copies of this book for your church, youth group, or civic organization from Amazon.com.

Special appreciation to Mark Snowden, neighbor, friend, and fellow minister for his help with this project.

Hear

Paul McCulley
Author of the award-winning book

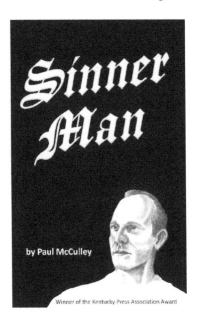

Winner of the Kentucky Press Association Award

- Heard worldwide on *"Unshackled"*
- Winner of the Kentucky Press
Association Award

An opportunity for youth and
adults to hear how God makes a
new man from a sinner man!

To contact Rev. Paul McCulley,
Email ***pmcculley@zoomtown.com***

Made in the USA
Monee, IL
17 September 2022